THE 2000 YEAR OLD MAN

by Mel Brooks
and Carl Reiner

Illustrated by
Leo Salkin

WARNER BOOKS

A Warner Communications Company

Warner Books, Inc.,
75 Rockefeller Plaza,
New York, N.Y. 10019

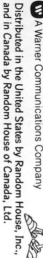 A Warner Communications Company

Distributed in the United States by Random House, Inc.,
and in Canada by Random House of Canada, Ltd.

Printed in the United States of America

First Printing: November 1981

10 9 8 7 6 5 4 3 2 1

Cover photograph of Mel Brooks by Nancy Andrews

Library of Congress Cataloging in Publication Data

Brooks, Mel.
The 2000 year old man.

Transcriptions from four sound recordings of
the authors.
    1. American wit and humor.   I. Reiner, Carl,
1922-   II. Title.
PN6162.B73   792.7028'0924   81-10297
ISBN 0-446-51238-9   AACR2

THE

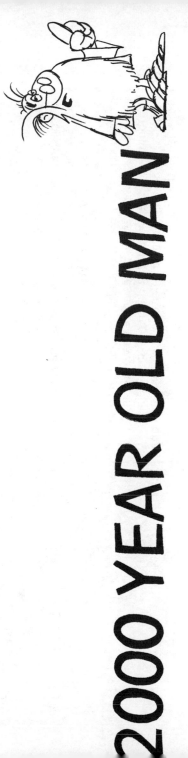

2000 YEAR OLD MAN

4

REINER: About four days ago a plane landed in Idlewild Airport. The plane came from the Middle East, bearing a man who claims to be two thousand years old. He spent the last six days at the Mayo Clinic. Sir, is it true that you are two thousand years old?

2000: Oh, boy. Oh, yes.

REINER: You are two thousand. It's hard to believe, sir, because in the history of man nobody has ever lived more than a hundred and sixty-seven years, as the man from Peru was claimed to be. But you claim to be two thousand.

2000: Yes. I'll be—I'm not yet—I'll be two thousand October 16. This month, yes.

REINER: You'll be two thousand. When were you born?

2000: When I was born—oh, close to two thousand—October 16 I'll be two thousand years young. We say young, you know, not to curse ourselves. So there was little groups of us sitting in caves and looking at the sun and scared, you know? We were very dumb and stupid. You want to know something? We were so dumb that we didn't even know who were the ladies. They was with us but we didn't know who they were. We didn't know who was the ladies and who was fellas.

REINER: You thought they were just a different type of fellas.

2000: Well, yes, just stronger or smaller or softer. The softer ones, I think, were ladies all the time.

REINER: How did you find out they were ladies?

2000: A cute fat guy, you could have mistaken him for a lady, soft and cute.

REINER: Who was the person who discovered the female?

2000: Bernie.

REINER: Who was Bernie?

2000: Bernie, one of the first leaders of our group.

REINER: And he discovered the female?

2000: Yes.

REINER: How did it happen?

2000: He said, "Hey, there's ladies here!"

REINER: I'm very interested to find out how Bernie discovered the woman. How did it come to pass?

2000: Well, one morning he got up smiling. He said, "I think there's ladies here!" I said, "What do you mean?" So he said, "Cause in the night I was thrilled and delighted." See? So then he went into such a story— it's hundreds of years later, I still blush.

REINER: Sir, could you give us the secret of your longevity?

2000: Well, the major thing, the major thing, is that I never ever touch fried food. I don't eat it, I wouldn't look at it, and I don't touch it. And I never run for a bus. They'll always be another. Even if you're late for work, you know, I never run for a bus. I never ran, I just strolled, jaunty-jolly, walking to the bus stop.

REINER: Well, there were no buses in the time of...

2000: No, in my time...

REINER: What was the means of transportation then?

2000: Mostly fear.

REINER: Fear transported you?

2000: Fear, yes. You would see...an animal would growl, you'd go two miles in a minute. Fear would be the main propulsion.

REINER: I think most people are interested in living a long and fruitful life, as you have.

2000: Yes. Fruit is good, too, you mentioned fruit. Yeah. Fruit kept me going for a hundred and forty years once when I was on a very strict diet. Mainly nectarines. I love that fruit. It's half a peach, half a plum, it's a hell of a fruit. I love it! Not too cold, not too hot, you know, just nice. Even a rotten one is good. That's how much I love them. I'd rather eat a rotten nectarine than a fine plum. What do you think of that? That's how much I loved them.

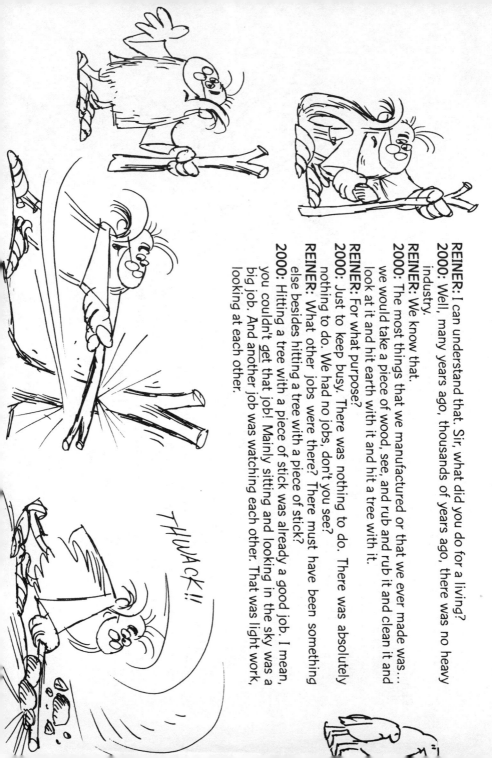

REINER: I can understand that, Sir, what did you do for a living?

2000: Well, many years ago, thousands of years ago, there was no heavy industry.

REINER: We know that.

2000: The most things that we manufactured or that we ever made was... we would take a piece of wood, see, and rub and rub it and clean it and look at it and hit earth with it and hit a tree with it.

REINER: For what purpose?

2000: Just to keep busy. There was nothing to do. There was absolutely nothing to do. We had no jobs, don't you see?

REINER: What other jobs were there? There must have been something else besides hitting a tree with a piece of stick?

2000: Hitting a tree with a piece of stick was already a good job, I mean, you couldn't get that job! Mainly sitting and looking in the sky was a big job. And another job was watching each other. That was light work, looking at each other.

THWACK!!

REINER: What language did you speak?

2000: They spoke Rock. Basic Rock.

REINER: That was before Hebrew?

2000: Yes, that was two hundred years before Hebrew, was the Rock language or Rock talk.

REINER: Could you give us an example of that?

2000: Yes: "Hey, don't throw that rock at me! Put that rock down! Hey, what are you doing with that rock there? I'll call a policeman, for God's sake! Put that rock away!" That was Rock.

REINER: Do you remember your Hebrew, sir?

2000: Yes, I think I remember it fluently.

REINER: Because, I understand, the modern Hebrew is different from the archaic.

2000: Yes. It differs in some of the phonetic alliterations and patterns.

REINER: Could we hear an example of the ancient Hebrew?

2000: The very ancient Hebrew is: "Oh, hi, there! Hello! Hello, there! How are you? I'm all right. How are you?"

REINER: That's English.

2000: Oh, wait. Wait.

REINER: Do you remember any Hebrew?

2000: Very little. I don't think I remember it. I must have forgot a great deal of it.

REINER: I think you forgot it all, sir.

2000: Maybe all, yes, maybe all. It's thousands of years since I needed it.

REINER: Sir, did you ever have any formal job as we know it today?

2000: Yeah, well, I was a manufacturer. I was an owner.

REINER: What kind of factory did you have?

2000: I used to make the Star of David. The Jewish stars. I was one of the first makers of that.

REINER: Oh, yes, the little thing you wear.

2000: As soon as religion came in, I was one of the first in that. I figured this was a good thing.

REINER: How did you make them, did you have tools?

2000: Well, we didn't have lathes. I employed six men, see, each with a point. And they used to run together in the middle of the factory and in their great speeds they would fuse the thing.

11

REINER: Thus making the Star.

2000: Yes. We would make two a day, because of the many accidents. You have six men running at high speeds with points, you know... plenty of accidents.

REINER: I see. You never thought of going into anything else?

2000: No. I had an offer once. A fellow came to me—Simon.

REINER: What did Simon ask you to do?

2000: He said, "We have a new thing, a new item, a winner, it looks like a winning item that's gonna be a big seller. It's called a cross." I looked at it and I turned it over and I looked at all sides of it and I said, "It's simple. It's too simple." I didn't know then it was eloquent. I didn't know it would be such a hit.

REINER: You turned him down?

2000: And I said, "I'm sorry, but I'm too busy." See, I could have fired four men—two men run together, bang!, we got a cross. I could have saved...I woulda had over a hundred dollars today if I'd went into crosses. They're in everywhere today.

REINER: By the way, sir, are you married?

2000: I've been married several hundred times.

REINER: Several hundred times! Do you remember all your wives?

2000: One I remember well.

REINER: Which one was that?

2000: The third one, Shirley. I remember her, a redhead.

REINER: I'm afraid to ask the next question. You've had many hundreds of wives—

2000: Hundreds and hundreds wives.

REINER: How many children do you have?

2000: I have over forty-two thousand children. And not one comes to visit me.

REINER: That's terrible.

2000: You bet. How they forget a father. Sure. That's how they are.

REINER: That's awful, sir. You mean to say there isn't one daughter that...

2000: Many daughters, but you know how they are, children. Good luck to them, let 'em go. I don't even—listen, let 'em be happy. As long as they're happy, I don't care. But they could send a note and write. "Hiya, Pop, how ya doin', Pop?" You know. Something. No, they don't.

REINER: Sir, you must have known some great men in your time. You did travel throughout the world.

2000: I knew the great and the near-great.

REINER: Could I ask you about some of these?

2000: Certainly. I'll tell you the truth whether I knew or not.

REINER: For instance, people are very interested in somebody like Joan of Arc. A lot has been written about her and...

2000: Ah, what a cutie! Joan of Arc!

REINER: You knew Joan of Arc!

2000: I went with her, dummy. I went with her!

REINER: Nowhere in history do we know of Joan going with anyone.

2000: Well, they don't print that. They don't print everything.

REINER: You didn't marry her.

2000: No, no, I didn't marry her because she was on a mission, you know. She used to say to me, "I gotta save France." I used to say, "Look, I gotta wash up. You save France, and I'll see ya later, after you save France and I wash up..." Her in her way, me in mine.

REINER: How did you feel about her being burned at the stake?

2000: Terrible. <u>Terrible.</u>

14

REINER: Sir, how about some of the legendary characters who supposedly might have existed? For instance, Robin Hood—did he exist?

2000: Oh, yeah, lovely man. Ran around in the forest.

REINER: Did he really steal from the rich and give to the poor?

2000: No. He didn't.

REINER: He didn't?

2000: He stole from everybody and kept everything. That's what he did.

REINER: Well, how did legend spring up that he was such a—

2000: He had a fellow, Marty—Marty the press agent—who ran in all the papers—he wrote in scrolls that he took from the rich and gave to the poor. Who knew? He gave you such a knock on the head when he robbed you that you wouldn't remember anything anyway. He was a tough guy.

REINER: I hate to have our legendary figures smashed like this.

2000: Well, I hate to smash 'em for you.

REINER: You've lived so long, did you ever have an accident in all this time?

2000: An accent? Always.

REINER: An accident.

2000: Oh, an accident. Yes. In the year sixty-one, I was run over by seven men fleeing a lion. They ran me over.

REINER: That's the extent of all...?

2000: But they didn't have insurance, I didn't have insurance. There was no such thing then. So you laid there till you got better.

REINER: It's amazing — in the two thousand years you've lived, you've seen a lot of changes.

2000: Yes. I certainly have.

REINER: What is the biggest change you've seen?

2000: In two thousand years, the greatest thing mankind ever devised, I think, in my humble opinion, is Saran Wrap. You can put a sandwich in it, you can look through it, you can touch it. You can put it over your face and fool around and everything. It's so good and cute! You can wrap it up. I love it. You can put three olives in it and make a little one; you can put ten sandwiches in it and make a big Saran Wrap. Whatever you want. It clings and it's great. You can look right through it.

REINER: You equate this with man's discovery of space?

2000: That was good. That was good. That was a good thing, space, finding space.

REINER: Sir, we don't have too much time, but we all here would like to know your Code.

2000: Well, all right. Is this it?

REINER: You're on.

2000: My farewell?

REINER: Your farewell address.

2000: OK....Hello dere! This is Two Thousand Years talkin' to you from the depths of back there when we was and now I'm still and they not. And I just wanna say, keep a smile on your face and stay out of a Ferrari or any small Italian car. Stay out of them. And I wanna tell you that it's been a wonderful two thousand years — and you've been a wonderful civilization — and it's been a thrill living for two thousand years — and eat a nectarine. It's the best fruit ever made.

(Six months later)

REINER: A few months ago a man came from the East who claimed to be two thousand years old. And since then many thousands of letters have come in asking us to put certain questions to him. His vast fund of information, his knowledge of the past, would be invaluable to historians throughout the world. So tonight we're in his comfortable suite in the Waldorf-Astoria. He's lounging on a chair and we're going to put some questions—

2000: (singing): "It's a lovvvely day today..."

REINER: It's so wonderful to see you, sir—how do you keep your spirits up?

2000: Oh, hello dere!

REINER: Hello, sir.

2000: I remember you from the last record. You keep yourself nice. You look nice. Yes.

REINER: Sir, if I may return the compliment—I am still under forty and you are two thousand and six months now—

2000: Two thousand and six months young. But I don't look more than sixteen, seventeen hundred, right?

REINER: No, you really don't. How do you keep this young, sir?

2000: Exercises keep me alive. I open the window —

REINER: Yes?

2000: And I'm in my nice shorts. A dollar twenty for Fruit of the Loom shorts. I inhale, then I exhale, then I inhale, then I exhale. Then I fall to my knees and pray fiercely for twenty-two minutes.

REINER: Twenty-two minutes of prayer every day has kept you alive?

2000: Yes, that a ceiling shouldn't fall on me or my heart should not attack me.

REINER: Your quaint language, sir, has caused me to laugh.

2000: That's my peppy ways.

REINER: Yes, you are a peppy person.

2000: I have very peppy ways.

REINER: Sir, you talked about your heart attacking you. I imagine in your life, two thousand years, you have had some sicknesses.

2000: Yes, I have had some sickness.

REINER: What is the worst thing that ever happened to you?

2000: I had a headache. You wanna hear about a headache?

REINER: I'd like to, sir.

2000: I hadda pull over to the side of the road. I threw away a new cigarette that I just lit up.

REINER: We have the new miracle drugs today to keep people alive. What did you have in your day to keep you healthy?

2000: We had our herbs. We took certain grasses, certain barks of certain trees which are not to be mentioned on this record.

REINER: Why is that?

2000: Because I don't want to throw the whole ethical drug field into chaos.

REINER: I see. I see.

2000: Everybody would go to certain trees, you know what I mean? Certain barks made you jump in the air and sing "Sweet Sue". Other barks of trees made you drowsy and sleepy and you were not to get on an animal and drive if you ate that bark.

REINER: How did you become a doctor in those days?

2000: In those days you went to a place.

REINER: What place?

2000: It was a very big cave.

REINER: Yes. And what was in that cave?

2000: An enormous cave and there was residents and interns. That was your first hospital. A big cave. And the same principles today, nineteen sixty—what are we?

REINER: One.

2000: Nineteen sixty-one. The very same principles that we had in the big caves are operating today in your major general metropolitan metropolis hospitals.

REINER: What are these principles?

2000: The principles are people walking past you when you're screaming— and not caring.

REINER: I see, sir.

2000: The same wonderful indifference to the sick and the dying. And we had that then. We invented that.

REINER: Sir, did you know King Arthur? Did he exist? Did you know him —
King Arthur and the Knights of the Round Table?

2000: King Arthur — a very important man. Wasn't only a king.

REINER: What do you mean?

2000: He owned four apartment buildings. He was some man, sure.

REINER: And the Knights of the Round Table existed?

2000: No Round Table.

REINER: No Round Table.

2000: No Round Table!

2000: No Round Table. Only when he ate with his family was it a round
table. When guests came — knights came — they would open it and put in
the leaves. They called him "King Arthur of the Oval Table."

REINER: Oh, I see, I see. And is it true that in those days the knights were
so gallant they would really fight for a lady's handkerchief?

2000: Oh, a handkerchief was one of the big fights. If you happened to
stumble on one of them terrible fights — when a lady would lose a handkerchief and two knights would go at each other on horsies, with long
spears, you know, and run at each other and go to kill each other to
get that handkerchief...

REINER: Why was that?

2000: Because there was no Kleenex.

REINER: I see.

2000: Once a Knight got that handkerchief, he blew his nose pretty good.

REINER: I see.

2000: I never had a handkerchief then.

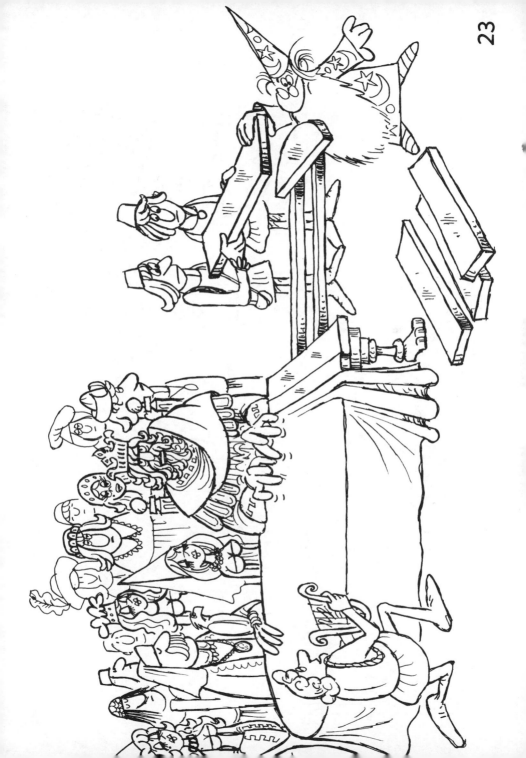

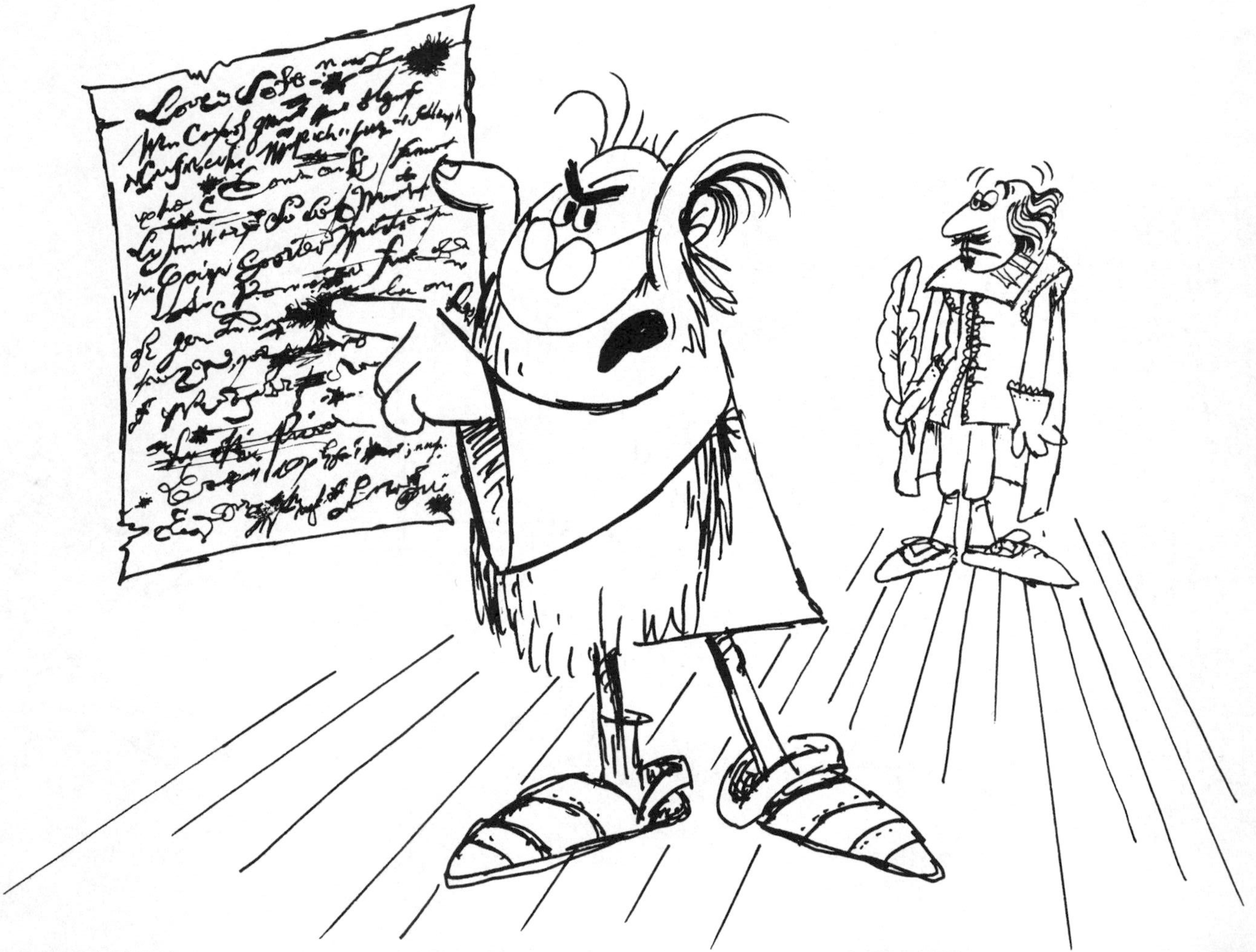

REINER: Well, I don't want to ask you about the origination of the handkerchief, but would you discuss with us, for instance, somebody like William Shakespeare?

2000: What a pussycat!

REINER: Are you saying that you knew him personally?

2000: What a pussycat! Oh, with that little beard, with that cute hair! Oh, was he good and smart! Oooh, was he smart!

REINER: It was reputed—and I guess you're agreeing—that he was the greatest writer of all time.

2000: Oh, no. Oh, no! Hey! Hold up. Hee haw. Whoa!

REINER: What do you mean, sir? You just said—

2000: A cute man and a pussycat—

REINER: But not a great writer?

2000: Not a good writer at all. Shakespeare was not a good writer. No.

REINER: How could you say that?

2000: He was a dreadful writer.

REINER: He wrote thirty-seven of the greatest plays—

2000: Did you ever see the originals, the First Folios?

REINER: You mean they were edited by someone else?

2000: Never mind edited. Did you see the Folios?

REINER: No, I never saw them.

2000: I saw the Folios. You wanna see how they were? With blots. With ink. With an "l" that looked like a "t." With an "m" you didn't know it was an "m." With an "o" could be a "p." Every letter was cockeyed and crazy. Don't tell me he was a good writer. He had the worst penmanship I ever saw in my life!

REINER: But he did, as it was reputed, he did write thirty-seven of the greatest plays of all—

2000: Thirty-eight.

REINER: I only knew of thirty-seven. Would you care to look at this list, sir?

2000: That is the list that has come down through the ages, yes.

REINER: That is the thirty-seven. Are there any others that should be there?

2000: Yes.

REINER: What's that?

2000: Queen Alexandra and Murray. Never heard of that, right?

REINER: No, I never did. Is there any copy of this in existence?

2000: This is a play that I invested money in.

REINER: Well, it probably was the only one that didn't come to light.

2000: Come to light? It closed in Egypt.

REINER: Well, sir, do you remember any of the dialogue of Queen Alexandra and Murray?

2000: Yes. Queen Alexandra turned to Murray and said, "What ho, Murray! What could it have been that I have seen? Is it not in my marrow? Are we not of one and ourselves?" And he would say to her, "What are you hollerin'? What are you hollerin'?"—

REINER: Sir, that doesn't sound to me—

2000: "—You'll wake up the whole castle!"

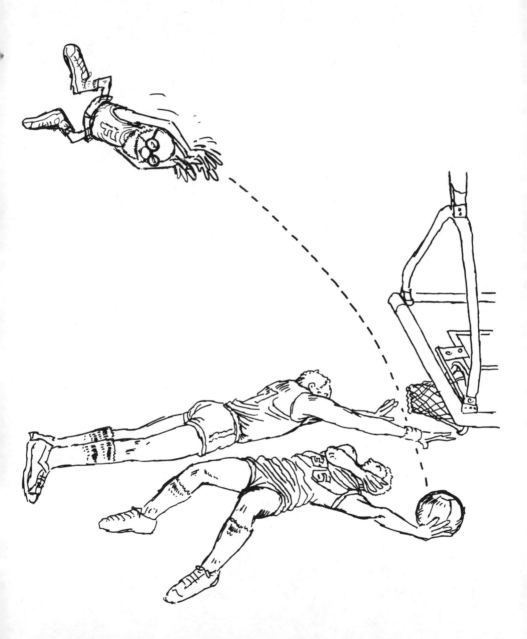

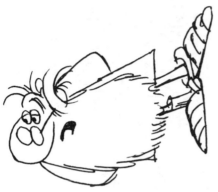

REINER: Sir, the father of modern psychiatry was Sigmund Freud.
2000: Sigmund Freud. He was a good basketball player. Very few people know that.
REINER: Sigmund Freud?
2000: Yes. He was short but he could dribble good.
REINER: I just saw a play on Freud and it wasn't suggested in the play at all.
2000: They left out the whole basketball?
REINER: They didn't discuss it at all.
2000: Oh, get out of here!
REINER: Really, sir.
2000: They don't mention it? He won his letter in that!
REINER: I thought he won his letter in medicine and literature.
2000: You see, why they don't mention it is because he used to set up the shots. He wouldn't take shots himself. That's why he was unnoticed in his greatest thing, basketball.

28

REINER: Sir, I'd like to find out about some social customs, the origination of social customs. For instance, singing. How did that start?

2000: Oh, it stems from fear.

REINER: Could you explain that?

2000: Because in the old days — and when I say the old days I don't mean the George M. Cohan days —

REINER: You mean two thousand years ago.

2000: I mean of rocks and caves.

REINER: Yes. I'm asking you, sir, how song came about...

2000: So, Song came about when you really had to communicate. When you were in trouble, you couldn't say "Help."

REINER: Yes.

2000: What the heck is saying "Help."?

REINER: Yes.

2000: You say, "Help," they say, "Hello." You know, they didn't hear you. You'd say "Help," they'd say "Good morning." So song started when you really had to—you were in trouble—you had to get somebody. You said, "He-e-e-l-l-l-pppl!!"

REINER: That was the first song.

2000: That's a note.

REINER: I see. So, in other words, fear caused...

2000: Yes, fear caused singing.

REINER: We thought happiness did.

2000: And the songs came out of it: "A lion is eating my foot off! Somebody call a cop! A lion is eating...." That's how song came about. Sure. The first songs, mind you, the first songs were only help songs. You wanna hear another help song?

REINER: How about an anthem?

2000: We had a national anthem.

REINER: What was the anthem?

2000: You see, it was very fragmented...

REINER: Yes?

2000: We wasn't nations.

REINER: Yes.

2000: We was caves.

REINER: Yes.

2000: Each cave...

REINER: ...was a nation.

2000: Each cave had a national anthem.

REINER: Yes. Do you remember the national anthem of your cave?

2000: I certainly do. I'll never forget! You don't forget a national anthem in a minute.

REINER: Let me hear it, sir.

2000: "Let 'em all go to hell except Cave 76!"

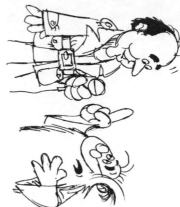

REINER: Sir, for instance, how did the custom of two people shaking hands—the handshake—come to be?

2000: The handshake, as you know—

REINER: I don't. That's why I'm asking.

2000: The handshake also stems from fear.

REINER: Everything seems to stem from fear.

2000: Well, of course. Everything we do is based on fear.

REINER: Even love?

2000: Mainly love.

REINER: How could love stem from fear?

2000: What do you need a woman for? You know what you need her for?

REINER: What?

2000: In my time?

REINER: Yes?

2000: To see if an animal is behind you. You can't see alone. You got no eyes in the back of your head. You take two eyes, happens to be a lady. You say, "Lady, will you look behind me for a while?" The first marriages was: "Will you take a look behind me?" "OK." "How long you want?" "Forever." "We're married."

REINER: And you'd walk back-to-back for the rest of your life?

2000: Yes. You only look at her once in a while.

REINER: When you knew you were safe.

2000: Yes. When you knew you were on high ground.

REINER: Let's get back to the handshake, sir. It started how? Through fear...?

2000: It started to see if a fellow had a rock or a dagger in his hand. You'd grab his hand. "Hi, there, Charlie! Ha ha...How ya doin', Bertram?"

REINER: That was very suspicious.

2000: You held that hand. And you looked and you opened it up and then you shook it a little.

REINER: And that's how the handshake started.

2000: You hadda shake. He may have had a stone in it. A small stone or a marble. He could stick it in your eye, you know what I mean? He could hold a rubber band there, could give you a smack in the nose.

REINER: How did dancing start?

2000: Dancing is the same thing.

REINER: Fear again?

2000: You see, the only thing you could do with a hand is to see if there was a rock or a marble or a rubber band or a nail or something that could stick it in your head. Right? Right. OK. But you're only immobilizing one hand. Dancing is the complete immobilization of both hands. And you keep the feet busy so they can't kick you. "Da da da, da da da...." Who's hurting you? Nobody's hurting you.

REINER: You have had many businesses, I know, and you've told us on your other record of what you've done for a living. You were a match-maker, I understand.

2000: Ah, yes! I brought wondrous people together.

REINER: Do we know any of the matches you've made,...the successful ones, say?

2000: Well, Madame Curie.

REINER: Madame and Doctor Curie?

2000: No, Madame Curie and Benjamin Franklin.

REINER: Now, just a moment. There's no record of Benjamin Franklin and Madame Curie ever having been —

2000: (Whistles)

REINER: Oh, well, sir, I see, I don't want to get into that. I don't want to get into that.

2000: What do you think, he flew a kite all night? And she liked him, too —

REINER: I don't want to fall to the level of —

2000: She gave him radium!

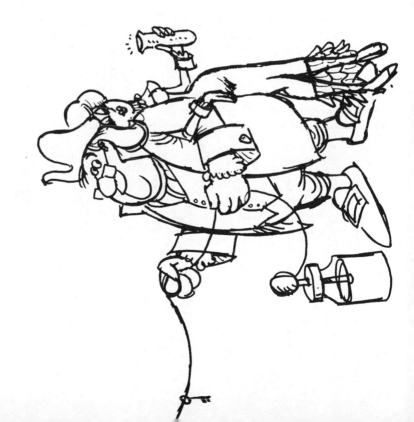

34

REINER: By the way, sir, did you know Napoleon?
2000: Short, right?
REINER: Yes. Did you know him?
2000: I didn't know him when he was a hit.
REINER: When did you meet him? Where did you meet him?
2000: I took a summer cottage in Elba.
REINER: Oh, I see, and you met him in Elba.
2000: And every day a shrimp used to go down by the water and cry.
REINER: You didn't know it was the great Napoleon?
2000: No, no.
REINER: Who did you think he was?
2000: A fellow in a bathing suit. How do I know? There was no place to
    put his hand. You know? How could you tell?
REINER: I understand you had an influence on him.
2000: Yes, I did have an influence. I said, "Look, they took France away
    from you. Why don't you go back and open your mouth and tell them
    who you are and what—"
REINER: So you're responsible for his demeanor?
2000: Well, I'm not responsible. You don't listen to every nut on a beach
    who tells you to go take France.
REINER: I see. It was his own fault.
2000: If a fellow came over to you and said, "Go back to France," would
    you go?
REINER: No.
2000: No. Right. He went. He's a dummy.

REINER: Sir, this is a world that is torn with strife. You, with all your knowledge, must be able to tell us how we all can be better citizens of the world.

2000: If every human being in the world would play a violin, we would be bigger and better than Mantovani!

(Two years later)

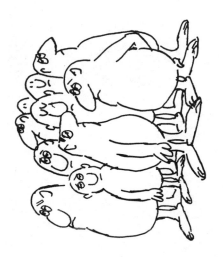

REINER: I'd like you to meet now a gentleman whom I've had the pleasure of meeting and interviewing two or three times before—the two thousand-year-old man!

2000: Hello dere!

REINER: Hi, sir.

2000: How are ya?

REINER: How are you, sir?

2000: Good to see you.

REINER: A lot of people still do not believe you are two thousand years old, but it has been authenticated.

2000: Yes, it has. Certainly. I have a birth certificate in the land of Ogg. But I don't carry my birth certificate around.

REINER: Why?

2000: Because it's a boulder, it's inscribed on a boulder.

REINER: Yes, that would be cumbersome.

2000: Credit cards, that's enough.

REINER: Sir, are there any more secrets that you're ready to divulge about how and why to live two thousand years?

2000: Well, one of the big things that's kept me rollin' along, singin' a song, is garlic.

REINER: Garlic has kept you alive? How can garlic keep you alive?

2000: Well, you know how you die, don't you? The scientific reason how you die is that the Angel of Death rings your apartment bell and you let him in and bang, you know. He comes in and says, "OK, Murray—this is it." And you go off in the night.

REINER: So how does garlic help?

2000: Usually comes at night, right?

REINER: Yes.

2000: So before I retire, I'll eat myself a nice pound and a half garlic, and then I lay down in bed and I pull up my crazy quilt and I'll start in to retire and snore.

REINER: And how does the garlic help?

2000: Well, the Angel of Death, you know, comes in, he comes over to me, he taps me on the shoulder and I say, "Who is it?" And he usually goes, "WHEW!!!" And he takes right off!

REINER: And he's out.

2000: He's out the door.

REINER: Well, that's an interesting theory.

2000: You know about the Kiss of Death, right?

REINER: Yes?

2000: Sure, he's not gonna kiss me! I'm full of garlic.

REINER: I see. Sir, what did you do two thousand years ago to entertain each other?

2000: A Buck and Wing.

REINER: No, no. Were there comedians?

2000: Oh, sure. Oh, sure.

REINER: Do you remember any of them?

2000: In primitive days — I remember one comedian, gave us some laugh. We were in hysterics.

REINER: Who was he?

2000: Murray the Nut.

REINER: What did he do?

2000: Oh! Did he give us a laugh! A tiger came in the cave one afternoon — sauntered in, uninvited, naturally, nobody asked for a tiger to walk in — a tiger came in, and Murray, you know, the joker, the tummler, you know, the nut, he jumps up and he grabs the tiger by the tail and he went, "Yaha! Yaha! Yaha!" And the tiger turned around and ate him up in a minute. And did we get <u>hysterical!</u> We were laughing….we were laughing from that joke! That was the best joke we ever had.

REINER: Well, sir, that's not very funny, that's rather —

2000: Well, did we have RKOs then? That was the best we had — Murray took a tiger on.

REINER: That was entertainment?

2000: Yes.

REINER: But I would consider that in the realm of tragedy rather than comedy. How do you differentiate between comedy and tragedy?

2000: Well, it's the point of view. To me, tragedy is if I cut my finger. That's tragedy. It bleeds and I'll cry and I'll run around and I'll go into Mount Sinai for a day and a half. I'm very nervous about it. And, to me, comedy is if <u>you</u> walk in an open sewer and die. What do I care?

REINER: You have seen many stage presentations in the two thousand years since the Greeks. Sir, what is the best and most interesting stage play you ever saw?

2000: Oh, what's the sense talking? Antony and Cleopatra. Can't beat it.

REINER: Which one? That's the one that Shakespeare wrote?

2000: What wrote? No wrote! Life! Real Life! I walked up in Egypt there and there was Antony and Cleopatra. We all took a look at them. That was the play. That's life.

REINER: That was the original cast.

2000: Yeah, the original cast, right.

REINER: But that wasn't a play. You weren't allowed to –

2000: We were allowed. They knew they were a hit. They let people see them kiss.

REINER: You mean they sold tickets to that?

2000: Well, they didn't sell tickets. You put a few drachmas in the pot when you went in.

REINER: Really? And did you know Cleopatra?

2000: Lovely woman.

REINER: Was she really twenty-one when she died?

2000: Get outta here! Twenty-one! What are you? A nut?

REINER: How old was she?

2000: Eighty-six. A nice age.

REINER: But why does history have it that she was twenty-one?

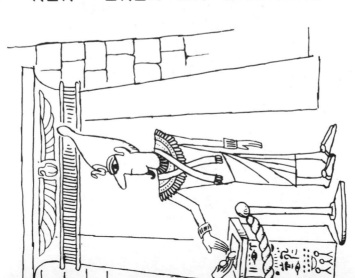

43

44

2000: History! They cook it up. And she didn't die from an asp either— no, sir!—you know, from a snake, that nonsense.
REINER: What was it?
2000: A stroke.
REINER: Oh.

2000: A stroke. They rushed her to the hospital pyramid and they pushed her around a little bit and she said, "Waugggghhh!" and died.
REINER: Those were her last words?
2000: Yes.

REINER: You have been around a lot, sir. Medicine must intrigue you.

2000: Yes. I happen to have been a physician myself.

REINER: You were a doctor?

2000: Oh, sure. I was a doctor for over one hundred years. I liked that for a while.

REINER: Why did you quit?

2000: I didn't know it would be popular again on TV. I woulda stuck with it.

REINER: What did you have to know to be a doctor in those days?

2000: The main thing you had to know is to say, "I think he's dead." You took a finger and put it in their nose. If they didn't say, "Hey, you take your finger out of my nose," they're dead. That's how you found out.

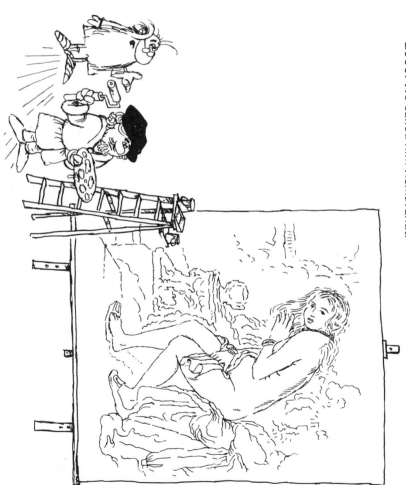

REINER: Sir, you must have known many great men in your time.
2000: I knew the great and the near-great.
REINER: Sir, did you know Rembrandt van Rijn?
2000: We called him Rembrandt.

REINER: You knew him?

2000: Yes. You know, Rembrandt was one of the first to use the roller.

REINER: The what?! How can you possibly...? The roller?! You mean the wall roller?

2000: Yes, the little roller, only for the backgrounds. Rembrandt didn't eat much, you know. The money always went for paint. An occasional girl, and then paint. Paint and paint and then a girl, then paint, then a girl, then paint. Then for a long time, just girls.

REINER: How about Michelangelo?

2000: How about him?

REINER: Is that all you care to say about him?

2000: Nice fella. Used to come in the store once in a while.

REINER: Michelangelo was one of your customers?

2000: Oh, a big customer.

REINER: Did he ever pay you off in a piece of art?

2000: We used to cuff him a lot.

REINER: What?

2000: Put him on the cuff. Painters never had money.

REINER: Well, did you think of taking a piece of his art? It would be worth—

2000: I thought it stunk. Who knew?

REINER: Why did you think that?

2000: Because it's all people flying around, you know. It wasn't like a nice picture of somebody on a pony. Those are nice.

REINER: They were naked, too.

2000: Yes, you can't hang a naked in your living room.

REINER: They do now.

2000: Well, now they're modern and dirty; then we were clean and cute.

48

REINER: Sir, have you ever been asked to spy?

2000: I spied for Washington.

REINER: For our country?

2000: Yes, for the father of our country, President George Washington. I not only was a spy for George, I was a counterspy.

REINER: I don't understand that. How can you —

2000: Well, we had a little restaurant in Valley Forge, I worked the counter and listened. I was a counterspy.

REINER: I see. Who did you listen to?

2000: Once in a while a Hessian would come in, you know. And I'd — you could hear that "Roch bachen, was ist gemacht." "I'd go, "Georrrrge — a Hessian!" He'd give 'em a smack on the head and that's it.

REINER: You were very close to the whole revolution, weren't you?

2000: Yes.

REINER: Did you know Benedict Arnold?

2000: I knew him and I despised him.

REINER: Because he was a traitor?

2000: No, because he told me he was gonna meet me that night and I'd have a date...

REINER: Did you know he was a traitor?

2000: The same night he was supposed to bring a girl for me he goes and betrays his country!

REINER: Sir, do you know the origin of some of our sports? Are you interested in sports at all?

2000: Well, tennis is a heck of a game.

REINER: Where did tennis start? In England, wasn't it?

2000: No, way before England. Tennis started in Egypt.

REINER: Did somebody invent it or was it accidental?

2000: No, in Egypt then it used to be skunks. A skunk would walk around near your pyramid, you take a stick, bang, you hit him away, right? But it heads for somebody else's pyramid, they don't want a skunk, bang, he hits it back to you. Well, you give the skunk, bang, another shot. Bang, bang, bang. And that was tennis.

REINER: I see. And people used to sit and watch it?

2000: Right. Then you'd jump over the skunk and shake hands.

REINER: Now, how did they get the term racquet? Why do they call it a tennis racquet?

2000: Oh, that comes because of Egypt. They used cat gut. Cats. There were many cats in Egypt, see, that's where they get the term "racquet."

REINER: How?

2000: Well, when you start taking the guts out of a cat, that's some racket there.

REINER: I see.

2000: You wanna hear a racket? Rrrragh! They scream pretty good. They don't give you their guts so easily.

REINER: Sir, you have vacationed, I guess, all over the world.

2000: Yes, I love vacations. I love to take a nice holiday.

REINER: What is your favorite resort of all?

2000: Europe. I keep a locker in Europe.

52

REINER: What advice would you give to the youth of the world to make this a peaceful, happy world?

2000: I would say to the children of the world: Listen to your mother and your father. Listen to your grandmother and your grandfather. Listen to an aunt and an uncle. Listen to a smart niece. Listen to a good-looking cousin. And mainly listen to your heart. And listen to your watch. And listen to your fountain pen. Listen to your inkwell. But never, never, ever listen to a fellow who comes over to you with pointy teeth. You know why? Because that's <u>Dracula!</u> And I don't want you to listen to him! He's no good. Goodbye, good luck.

(Thirteen years later)

REINER: In nineteen hundred and sixty a phenomenon came to the attention of the world. A man claiming to be two thousand years old was proven by our foremost medical authorities to be just that. His wisdom has been a great source of inspiration to those of us who have had the privilege to know him. He's back in Los Angeles at this time for his Bicentennial checkup, and he has consented to honor us with his revered and distinguished presence. Ladies and gentlemen, the Two-Thousand-and-Thirteen-Year-Old man.

2000: Thank you.

REINER: Sir, how are you?

2000: Thank you, thank you.

REINER: How are you feeling?

2000: I'm all right.

REINER: Sir, you are now looking,
I must say, not any older
than you did ten years ago.
You are now two thousand
thirteen. What has kept you
alive?

2000: Will Tolive.

REINER: Ah, yes, the will to live.

2000: Not the will to live. Doctor Tolive! Doctor Will Tolive. The man
that's kept me alive. William Tolive. A genius. The man's a genius.

THIS CERTIFIES
WILL TO LIVE, M.D.

55

REINER: One of the great geriatric specialists has a theory that was printed just a while ago that your long life may be attributed to the slowness of your heartbeat and the slowness of your development. Were you a slow developer as a child?

2000: Yes. Verrrry slow. He's right, he's right. Because an elephant is slow — lives long.

REINER: That's right.

2000: A turtle is slow — lives long.

REINER: That's right. So as a youth you were slow?

2000: I started everything low and slow. I breastfed for two hundred years.

REINER: Really?

2000: Yes.

REINER: Oh, now, now, now, sir...did you?

2000: Yes. I loved it. I look back on that as the happiest part of my life, I'll tell you the truth.

REINER: Sir, who did you breastfeed with? Who breastfed you?

2000: I used to con a lot of ladies into doing it. They took pity on me. Oh, it was a thrill, let me tell you.

REINER: What other parts developed slowly?

2000: Well, it took me two hundred years before I got my public hair.

REINER: You mean your chest hair and your genital hair.

2000: My what?

REINER: Your hair around your private parts.

2000: We don't say genital, we say our gentle, our gentle parts. You have to be very gentle there.

REINER: That's not called public hair, it's called pubic hair.

2000: No, I got my pubic hair when I was about fifteen or sixteen, I'm talking my public hair. The hair on your chest, on your arms, your head, your feet, the hair the public can see. Not private.

REINER: Sir, what was your diet like two thousand years ago?

2000: Two thousand years ago we only ate what God meant. The organic. The natural.

REINER: Like what?

2000: Clouds. Stars. Rocks. We ate big things.

REINER: Yes, but there was no nutrition in it.

2000: Well, you don't know. Many parts of a pine tree are edible—did you know that?

REINER: Oh, yes, I've heard of that.

2000: Yes, and did you know that pussy willows make a lovely dessert?

REINER: No, I didn't know that.

2000: Oh, sure, sure.

REINER: What else did you eat besides pussy willows?

2000: Oh, yes, you could eat insects too, but, you know—

REINER: Did you eat insects?

2000: Yes. You have to be careful of the red ant, because they're hard to kill. So if a few live ones are on your tongue, they'll eat your tongue before you'll eat them.

REINER: I see.

2000: You have to be very fast with the red ants to eat them. Because it's more or less a race with them —who eats who, you know? They're very quick.

REINER: You obviously don't eat red ants and rocks today,…

2000: No, no…

REINER:…because you can avail yourself of the foods that exist.

2000: Two thousand thirteen years old, I have to be verrrry careful.

REINER: What does your diet consist of today?

2000: Very strict. Very strict diet. Very strict. Almost nothing. No starches. No starches.

REINER: No starches?

2000: No, sir. Because starch turns to sugar, sugar turns to diabetes, diabetes turns to the grave.

REINER: I see, starches are out.

2000: No starches. No meats, because meats are fat and fat is cholesterol.

REINER: And fowl?

2000: No fowl.

REINER: And fowl?

2000: No fowl.

REINER: No fowl?

2000: Fowl is foul. You don't eat fowl. No good for you. Chickens eat crap.

REINER: No starches, no fowl, no meats…what about fish?

2000: No fish. Fish are iodine. Too much iodine, you get a goiter, your eyes'll spring out of your head. You have to be careful. You don't want it. No. No, sir.

REINER: Then, naturally, you live on vegetables.

2000: No, fruits and vegetables are very bad. Very bad. They're roughage and they make tons and tons of gas. And I have to be very careful because if I make

a bloozer I could blow myself out of this world. No gas. I'm not allowed to have gas.

REINER: Yes, at your age you're very brittle. I understand that. So you have nothing to eat, then. You've left yourself nothing to eat.

2000: Cool mountain water. Ten degrees below room temperature. Just cool mountain water.

REINER: And that's all you eat?

2000: Just that.

REINER: That's all you eat all day?

2000: That and a stuffed cabbage. That's all I eat. That's all I live on.

REINER: Is that allowable on your diet? Is stuffed cabbage allowable?

2000: Who the hell cares if it's allowable? I love it! What am I going to live for? For a little mountain water, you think I'm going to stay alive? Are you crazy?

REINER: Did you live before man believed in the Almighty?

2000: Oh, yeah, a few years before. A couple of years.

REINER: Did you believe in anything? Did you believe in any Superior Being?

2000: Yes, a guy, Phil.

REINER: Who was Phil?

2000: Phillip. The leader. The leader of our tribe.

REINER: What made him the leader?

2000: Very big. Very strong. A big beard, a big chest, and big arms. I mean, he could kill you. He could just walk on you and you could die.

REINER: And you revered him?

2000: We prayed to him. Would you like to hear one of our prayers to Phillip?

REINER: Could you remember these prayers?

2000: "Ohhhh, Phillip. Please don't take our eyes out and don't pinch us and don't hurt us. Ohhhhhh. Aaaaamen." That was it.

REINER: And Phillip did these things for you?

2000: Yes.

REINER: And you followed him?

2000: Right.

REINER: How long was his reign?

2000: Oh, not too long. Not too long. Because one day Phillip was hit by lightning.

REINER: Aaahh.

2000: And we looked up, we said, "There's something bigger than Phi-i-ll!"

REINER: So you gave up on Phillip.

2000: Yes.

REINER: And you started to pay allegiance to that new God.

2000: Yes, to the new Lord.

REINER: You didn't call him Lord then?

2000: No. The first name we had for him, I think, was Gevalt. Gevalt!
I mean, with lightning we were already gevalt! Wow!
REINER: I think that's an old Hebraic word meaning "My Goodness!"
2000: Yes, "My Goodness." At first Gevalt, and then there was —
REINER: How did it come to "God"?
2000: Gevalt, and Gevoo, Yaywah, and Yahweh. Yaywah, then Yahweh, then
Yourway, then Hisway, then Yahweh....
REINER: Jehovah.
2000: Yes. Yes.
REINER: And then to Lord.
2000: Then the Lord. Yes.

REINER: You know something, this world of ours if full of mysteries. What phenomenon intrigues you more than any other in this world?

2000: That's a hard question, because there's so many different phenomenon that—I'll tell you one that's very private, if you promise everybody here will keep their mouths shut. I'll say one phenomena that really puzzles me, a mystery that I—I don't want to talk about but I'll say it anyway.

REINER: Go ahead. You're among friends.

2000: All right. After I eat asparagus and I make Number One, there's such an odor. You know? Such a nutty flavor. I mean, that really puzzles me, why there should be that —

REINER: That must be some chemical reaction.

2000: I mean, it's frightening.

REINER: You know what intrigues me? The origin of words. You knew Shakespeare, you told us...he invented words.

2000: Yeah, he was cute, that pussycat with a beard.

REINER: How did the word "shower" come to be?

2000: Oh, "shower." Most words come out of onomatopoetica.

REINER: You mean they sound like what they are. Well, "shower" doesn't exactly sound —

2000: Well, listen, you go in a shower and you hear "s-s-s-s-s..."

REINER: But that's not "shower."

2000: Well, when they added the hot water, then you walked in and you went "Ouch!" It was "ouch-show-show...shower!" That's how we got "shower."

REINER: Simple. Simple. You mean all words, you think, are onomatopoetically based?

2000: All words basically come from the sound.

REINER: What about "egg"? "Egg" doesn't sound like an egg.

2000: Watch a chicken. Look at a chicken, study a chicken very, very, very, closely as it produces an egg. You listen to it and you'll see the chicken go "E-e-e-g-g-g-g-g..." and plop, an egg comes out.

REINER: I think I'm going to trip you up. Why do they call a nose a nose?

2000: What are you going to blow? Your eyes? Makes sense to me.

REINER: All right.

2000: Perfectly sensible.

REINER: Sir, what great inventors or discoverers do you feel our civilization is most beholden to? People like Pasteur come to my mind—
2000: He was good.
REINER: Columbus, Einstein...
2000: He was good. They were good.
REINER: Who do you feel were the great contributors to our civilization as we know it today?
2000: Jewish or anybody?
REINER: Anybody. Anybody.
2000: You left out Murray.
REINER: Murray?
2000: Murray was a hell of an inventor, one of the big inventors.
REINER: What did he invent?
2000: Fire.
REINER: Really? How did that come about?
2000: He was standing under a tree, and came a big bolt of lightning, set the tree on fire, and set Murray's beard and his clothes and his hair on fire. And he came running into the cave all on fire. And I jumped up. I remember I leapt to my feet, and I said, "Get your marshmallows on your sticks! Hurray! Hurray!" And then we all rushed at Murray, but we were so greedy we put him out. Too many marshmallows put out Murray. It was a terrible experience.
REINER: Well, you might have been unhappy, but I think Murray probably was happy. What other inventors were there besides Murray?

2000: Onan.
REINER: Onan? What did Onan invent?
2000: Onan discovered himself. A very big invention.
REINER: Yes, I see.
2000: I think he was falling and he grabbed onto himself and that's how he fell in love.
REINER: And he stayed with himself.
2000: And he lived with himself and he was in love.
REINER: Was he ostracized for being that way?
2000: He was circumcised. I don't know ostracized.
REINER: No, no, I mean was he shunned?
2000: Oh, yes, he was shunned because the Bible, it says, "Thou shalt not spill the seed of thy fruit on the ground," you know.
REINER: That's right, and also that "thou shalt be fruitful and multiply."
2000: And he was fruitless and subtracting, if you want to look at it that way.
REINER: Actually you're saying something that is very interesting. Because many guilts have been carried by many people because of Onan. He really was the inventor of masturbation.
2000: Shut up!
REINER: What?
2000: Hey! What's the matter with you? Teenagers are going to hear this!
REINER: Yes, but the word "masturbation"—
2000: Don't say that! You don't have to say that!
REINER: But in today's world—

2000: Don't say that word! There are other ways to imply — be oblique, be subtle. Don't say it. Be smart. Be smart.

REINER: That may be one of the problems —

2000: Can't you be clever? What the hell's the matter with you?

REINER: That's one of the problems that exist in the world today, because we use euphemisms.

2000: Yes, I understand that.

REINER: Instead of saying "masturbation" —

2000: Oh, get another question!

REINER: What things annoy you about our modern society? Now, many people feel that the thing that's most upsetting to them is that individual rights, the freedoms, are being taken away...

2000: Yes, our rights, our freedoms.

REINER: Do you feel that?

2000: Yeah. More important than that is they're taking away our smells. Our own individual smells. They have a spritz, they have a spray for everything. Under the arms, in the nose, in the crotch — you don't know who the hell you're talking to anymore! You don't know the difference between men and women, between who's who. Everybody smells like a strawberry. You walk past a fruit stand, you get hot. What the hell is that? That's no way to live! You can't lead your life that way!

REINER: It's upsetting.

2000: Sure, it's ridiculous.

REINER: Do you avail yourself today of the modern miracle medicines?

2000: I don't take drugs. I don't like drugs.

REINER: Don't use any drugs?

2000: I don't use drugs.

REINER: Well, what do you use instead of drugs if you have some illness or disease?

2000: Fruits. Fruits. The elixir of life.

REINER: You mean fruits can cure diseases?

2000: There's a fruit for any disease that mankind has had.

REINER: That's hard to believe.

2000: Name the disease, I'll give you the fruit.

REINER: Really?

2000: Absolutely.

REINER: Arteriosclerosis.

2000: Bananas.

REINER: Bananas?

2000: Bananas, 'cause arteriosclerosis is hardening of the arteries, you need something soft. Either bananas or a mushy pear. Either one will save you.

REINER: How about tuberculosis?

2000: Blueberries.

REINER: How? Why?

2000: They stain the tubercular bacteria, you find 'em, you kill them. Blueberries. Very good.

REINER: Diarrhea.

2000: Diarrhea, you gotta eat peaches. Peaches are very good for diarrhea.

REINER: Peaches? Any kind of peaches?

2000: Oh, no. Not Alberta.

REINER: Not Alberta?

2000: No. The cling peaches. They hold it together a little better.

72

REINER: Sir, what do you consider to be the greatest medical discovery in the two thousand years that you've lived? Would it be the advent of transplants of organs? The use of antibiotics? The heart-lung machine?

2000: Liquid Prell.

REINER: Liquid Prell.

2000: Now wait a minute—

REINER: Liquid Prell. Let me explain....

2000: You think it's a more important discovery than the heart-lung machine?

REINER: OK, the heart-lung machine is in your medicine cabinet and falls out, it's gonna break, right?

2000: Yes.

REINER: Liquid Prell don't break!

2000: It's in a plastic bottle.

REINER: Right. And what about the psychological aspects?

2000: What psychological aspects?

REINER: The <u>psychological</u> aspects...

REINER: There are no psychological aspects...

2000: ...of Liquid Prell....

REINER: ...it's a <u>shampoo</u>!

2000: Get out of here! What's the matter with you? Don't you see what it's doing? It's bringing families together! A mother of forty-two and a daughter of sixteen are talking for the first time! Don't you see? "Oh, Mom, oh, Mom, don't use too much..." "Oh, don't worry, it's concentrated." They <u>talk</u> to each other! Bringing the generations, bringing families together!

REINER: That's the beginning of a relationship, huh?

2000: Oh, sure, sure. Entire families are being held together with Liquid Prell. We owe a great debt to it. And it's green. If you put a pearl in it and hold it upside down, it goes verrrry slow.

REINER: You obviously like that Prell.

2000: I love it.

REINER: Sir, since you have lived through two millennia, I'm hoping that you have chronicled your life in biographies, autobiographies...

2000: Nah, nah, I never wrote any of my adventures down.

REINER: You didn't write any of this down? That's so sad!

2000: Nah, it's egotistical. It's egotistical.

REINER: Oh, yes, but after you've lived more than one thousand years you should have realized you were very special and should have done some writing.

2000: I did a little. A little writing.

REINER: What kind?

2000: A little poetry.

REINER: Poetry?

2000: Yeah. A little private poetry.

REINER: You are a romantic.

2000: I love poetry.

REINER: Yes, would you recite it?

2000: ...the shorthand of beauty, poetry, I love it.

REINER: Would you recite some of the poetry?

2000: I wrote it many years ago. I don't know if you would understand it. I'll take a shot. You want to hear?

REINER: Yes.

2000: "Nog, nog, mikel and bebob/ Feluch matuch meluch mitag."

REINER: That's a language I've never heard. It's not Hebrew.

2000: You know Sanskrit?

REINER: No, I don't.

2000: You know Cuneiform?

REINER: No.

2000: It's neither of those.

REINER: Oh, well...

2000: It's a very tough language.

REINER: What is it called? Does it have a name, this language?

2000: It's the Sand language.

REINER: We don't understand. It had a nice rhythm to it.

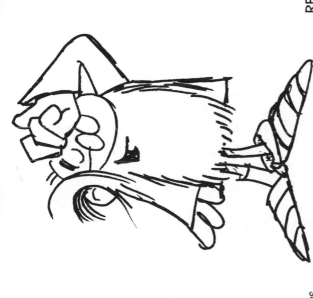

2000: Yes.
REINER: Is there a translation? Is it a romantic poem? Is it a romantic poem? I guess all poems are basically romantic.
2000: I could say it to you in English if you want to hear it. It loses all the beauty. All the gorgeousness, all the wonder, is gone....
REINER: Yes, the romance of a language is—
2000: But I'll say it if you want to hear it in English.
REINER: Well, give us the best romantic translation you can.
2000: "Beans, beans, the musical fruits,/The more you eats, the more you toots..." That's the poem in English.

REINER: Oh, did you write that?
2000: My best work!
REINER: Well, I'm in the mood of hearing the old Hebraic chants....
2000: Oh....
REINER: ...that the shepherds and the...
2000: Mmmmm....
REINER: ...and the people that sat on the hillside...
2000: Mmmmm....
REINER: ...singing...
2000: Mmmmm....
REINER: Do you remember any of those?
2000: Mmmmm...no, I don't.

REINER: Sir, how did you dress back in the old days, two thousand years ago? We see pictures on walls, and the legend has it that the fig leaf was the first wearing apparel.

2000: No, no.

REINER: The fig leaf wasn't?

2000: No, no, no, and no! It was not the first apparel. No, sir.

REINER: What was?

2000: The hat.

REINER: You mean man wore a hat on his genitals?

2000: Not on his genitles. He didn't wear a hat on his genitles! He wore a hat on his head, like you're supposed to wear a hat!

REINER: But that wouldn't protect your genitals.

2000: No. It's more important to protect the brain, and primitive man, he knew the brain...if God and nature intended that the gentles were more important than the brain, He would have put a skull over the gentles, and we knew that. So let's face it. Look, we're all adults. Let's talk plain. What the hell do you care if somebody comes over and fools around with you in your gentles? What the hell do you care? What is it? It's a momentary thing, right? It's there and it's gone, right? But you don't want anybody coming over and stroking your brains. You don't want that. 'Cause they'll scramble your brains, you'll write the wrong check out, you lose money. That's important. That stuff is important.

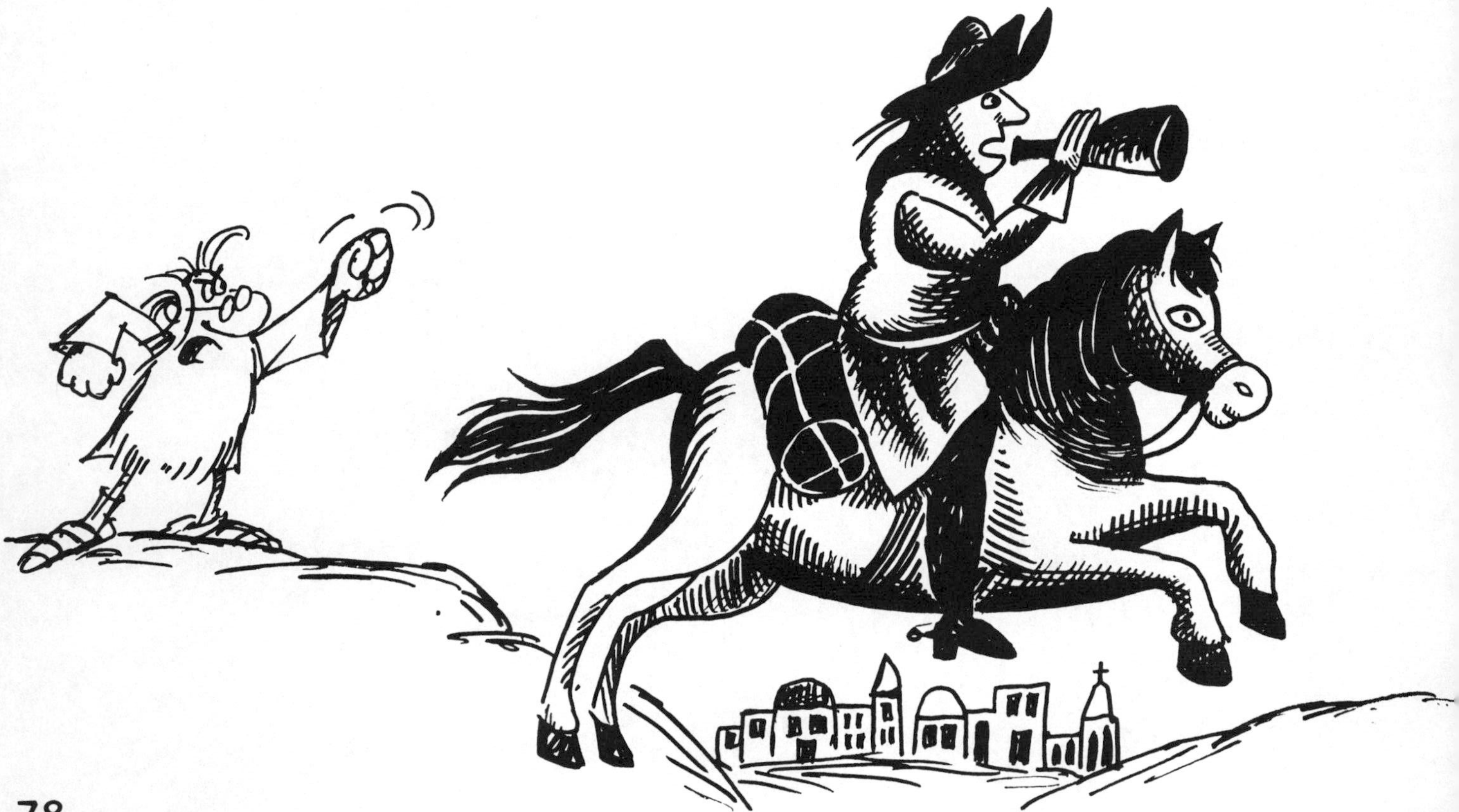

REINER: Sir, I read somewhere that you lived in Boston during the American revolution. Did you know Paul Revere?

2000: An anti-Semite bastard.

REINER: You didn't like Paul Revere?

2000: He hated the Jews.

REINER: He was a hero!

2000: No, he hated the Jews. I couldn't take him.

REINER: No, no, he was a hero! How could you call him an anti-Semite?

2000: He warned us, he was afraid they were moving in, he had fear that they were going in the neighborhood, to move in. "They're coming! They're coming! The Yiddish are coming!" All night he was yelling, "Beware of the Jews!"

REINER: Were you living in that neighborhood at the time?

2000: I was there, I heard him myself.

REINER: He was yelling, "The British are coming."

2000: Oy, my God! Oh! "The British are coming???"

REINER: And you moved out!

2000: Oh. Ooooh. I'm gonna have to send his wife a note. Oh! Oh. Oh. That is bad. I didn't know it. And I didn't go to his funeral! Oh, my God! What an error!

REINER: For two hundred years you maligned the man.

2000: Oh, I'm glad we spoke! I'm glad we spoke.

REINER: We should talk about some more of these people.

2000: Oh, wait, let me recover, wait. Ooooh.

REINER: Could you tell me about your mother and father?

2000: My mother and father were Jewish.

REINER: I imagined, yes.

2000: They're typical. Eternal. They're typical and eternal.

REINER: Now, wait, this goes back over two thousand thirteen years ago...

2000: I'm gonna tell you a nice thing. I'm gonna tell you the truth about all the Jewish mothers and fathers and the Jewish in-laws.

REINER: You're talking about your...?

2000: Mine and all. This is the truth about them. They all are prideful and spiteful and they all...for instance, I mean, when I was a kid, when I got married, it was in caves. Caves. Caves.

REINER: You were living in a cave and your parents came to dinner?

2000: We made dinner, we said, "Pa, Ma, come over, come over, come over for dinner." You know the Jewish mothers and fathers, they came over, it was a terrible rainstorm, they're standing outside the cave. I said, "Come in, Pa." "No, I'm all right here."

REINER: You mean he was standing outside the cave?

2000: "No, I'm fine, I'm fine." I said, "Pa, it's raining! Ma, it's raining on you!" "No, we all right. We don't have to come in. We just wanted to look at you." I mean, they're nuts!

REINER: Finally, what brought them in?

2000: So finally we pushed them in. "Could we take your coat? Let me take your coat." "No, it's all right. I'll keep my coat." "Sit down." "No, standing is good." "Sit down, we made dinner for you." "No, we ate. We ate on the dinosaur on the way over." They don't do nothing for you!

REINER: What was the reason...? Why is that? Why do they do that?

2000: Who knows? Jews are nuts.

REINER: You lived, of course, during the time of Christ...

2000: I knew Him. A nice boy.

REINER: You knew Jesus?

2000: Oh, He was nice. Lovely. Thin. A nice little beard. He wore sandals.

REINER: He wore sandals...very much as He's pictured today in the motion pictures that we see of Him?

2000: Well, they made a travesty of it—the throwing over the tables and knocking over things...

REINER: Well, didn't Jesus behave that way?

2000: No, He was quiet. A quiet lad.

REINER: He didn't do that?

2000: No. He came in the store—He never bought anything.

REINER: Oh, you had a store. Oh, I see. You were a merchant. By the way, did you know any of the Apostles?

2000: I knew them all. Sure. They came in the store.

REINER: You knew them well.

2000: Absolutely.

REINER: Could you tell us a little about them? Who were they?

2000: There was Ben. Murray. Al. Richie. Sol. Abe...

REINER: No, no, no, that's not the Apostles.

2000: Oh, wait. That's the William Morris Agency. Wait. It's the same stuff, you know.

REINER: Sir, is there anything you want to tell us about Jesus that we don't know that we should know? Because the history and mystery of Jesus is really one of the most fascinating things in the history of man.

2000: He was a carpenter.

REINER: We know that.

2000: Oh, that's all I had left.

REINER: So there's nothing new you can—

2000: No, no, I thought I'd shed that new light, but you all know it now.

REINER: Was He a good carpenter?

2000: The best.

REINER: Did He ever do anything for you?

2000: He made a cabinet for me.

REINER: Really? What kind of cabinet?

2000: Three drawers and two little drawers at the top.

REINER: Yes? And how much did He charge for it?

2000: Four drachmas.

REINER: How much was a drachma?

2000: A drachma's about a half a buck today.

REINER: Did you know at the time that Jesus was building you this cabinet?

2000: Sure. I paid Him. I wrote out a check to Jesus. I knew it.

REINER: But did you know He was going to be the Jesus who would shape the world?

2000: Are you kidding? If I knew it was going to be Him, I would have made Him a partner in the store. Who knew it was going to be a hit?

84

REINER: Sir, I'm always fascinated when you tell us personal things about the great historical figures. One intrigues me—General Custer.

2000: A FAG.

REINER: Wait a moment. Now just a moment—

2000: The man was a FAG.

REINER: We're talking about General Custer. He was a <u>general.</u>

2000: Hey, I was there, Charlie.

REINER: Are you saying that a general could be a fag?

2000: He's a FAG.

REINER: A general's a fag?

2000: <u>All</u> generals.

REINER: All generals? Just a moment. Are you trying to prove a psychiatric point?

2000: I'm saying the simple truth. What's so hard to understand?

REINER: Maybe <u>one,</u> but not all...

2000: Name the generals, I'll tell you.

REINER: George Washington?

2000: A FAG. The biggest.

REINER: General Eisenhower?

2000: A FAG.

REINER: General Cornwallis?

2000: A FAG.

REINER: General Patton?

2000: A big FAG.

REINER: Just how can you explain that, sir? None of these men seem, we haven't any history of them being, homosexuals.

2000: Hey, wait a minute! Hold on, pal. I didn't say <u>homosexual.</u> No. Don't get me in trouble.

REINER: You said these generals were fags.

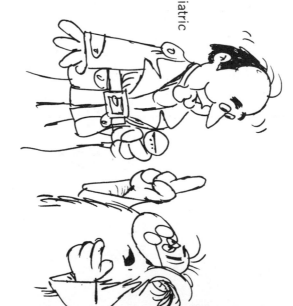

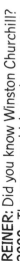

85

2000: Yes — Federal <u>Army</u> <u>Generals</u>. I didn't mean anything dirty. I don't want to take the time on the record to—I've shortened things, that's all.

REINER: You almost got us in a lot of trouble there.

2000: Yes. You bet. Homosexual!

REINER: Do you know any homosexuals?

2000: Maybe Custer. Could have been. He had long hair and he liked nice horses. Who knows?

REINER: Did you know Winston Churchill?

2000: The war would have been over four years earlier if it wasn't for Winston Churchill.

REINER: He prolonged the war, you say?

2000: Prolonged it four years, a good four years.

REINER: Why, by bad generalship?

2000: No, bad elocution. Because he said, "We must conquer the Narzis."

REINER: Yes.

2000: Now we were fighting and killing Nazis. We all left, we all went away and we were looking for Narzis. And there were no Narzis! Four years chasing Narzis! He should have said "Nazis." It would have ended the war.

REINER: But, I think very few people were confused by that.

2000: The man didn't talk good. That's because he sipped a few brandies.

REINER: Yeah, but how many people were confused by "Narzis"?

2000: Me. Well, me and my group. There was eight of us. We could have helped. We could have pitched in. It would have ended the war.

REINER: Your feeling about war—I would like to get that. Your feeling about war and the possibility that man will someday outgrow his need for using it to solve his problems.

2000: I hate it.

REINER: You hate war.

2000: I hate it.

REINER: Were you involved in—

2000: Every one.

REINER: Every war?

2000: I was in every war! Every war I joined up. That flag, those songs... I was a kid. I didn't know better. "Over There"—you know what the real song should be from war?

REINER: Can you sing it?

2000: "Let's go out and lose an eye/Let's lose a foot/Let's go to war and lose our brains." That should be the real song. They make nice songs.

REINER: Yes, I see. "Over There" gets you over there.

2000: And I was wounded and I was hurt. Half of me is plastic, the other half is a tin can. There's nothing left from war. I'm a shell of myself.

REINER: So there has never been a good war.

2000: One good war. There was. An exception.

REINER: Which one? The war for liberation?

2000: No, none of that bullshit. No, no.

REINER: The Revolutionary War? The Russian Revolution?

2000: No, there was one good war. The War of the Roses was a good war.

REINER: The War of the Roses in England?

2000: Yes, it was a just war.

REINER: A just war? What made that a just war?

2000: Well, Wednesday night we went to sleep, Thursday morning we woke up, there wasn't a rose in the country.

REINER: Somebody stole the roses.
2000: Came in, they took every rose.
REINER: Oh, I can't believe that.
2000: And, you know, we didn't smell too good, we needed the roses. So Thursday morning we went to war, we got back every rose. To hell with it. That was a just war. The only war worth fighting. Yes, sir. That war I'd fight again. Don't take my roses, mister! No, sir.

REINER: We do know that you have always been a romantic individual.

2000: Ahhh...

REINER: Four hundred wives will attest to that.

2000: A thousand violins explode in my mind. Yes. Wonderful. Constant.

REINER: Could you tell us — is this being too personal? — could you tell us the most unforgettable romantic interlude in your life?

2000: Oh, well, I don't know if I should say here. I don't know.

REINER: Come on. I think we'd all gain from it...

2000: It's private.

REINER: ...we'd all gain from it to know what a man of your stature feels as a romantic interest.

2000: Ah, what the hell, OK.

REINER: Who and when and what?

2000: Dolly Madison.

REINER: You dallied with Dolly Madison?

2000: Very well put. Yes.

REINER: You mean James Madison's wife?

2000: He was busy in the West Wing of the Oval House writing the Monroe Doctrine.

REINER: Well, just a moment...

2000: And he never paid attention to her. He was very busy.

REINER: Yes, well, just a moment...

2000: She had needs. The woman had needs. I had to satisfy the needs!

REINER: Just to keep this historically accurate, which we should do, you're talking about James Madison doing the Monroe Doctrine. I think you mean James Monroe.

2000: Then maybe it was Dolly Monroe. Wait.

REINER: I don't think Monroe's wife was named Dolly. I don't know what her name was.

2000: Who was the girl made the ice cream?

REINER: That was Dolly Madison.

2000: It was Dolly Madison. Because, I remember, we got hot, we fell right in the ice cream. We didn't know what we were doing. A tub of ice cream. It was Dolly Madison. My tush was cold for three days. You don't forget. You don't forget a thing like that.

REINER: I'm a little queasy about this, telling tales about Presidents and Presidents' wives.

2000: They're all a little wacky, the Presidents. They're a little power-crazy, right? And they love to do it. Let's face it. They love it. They LOVE it.

REINER: Yes.

2000: And if they don't do it to their wife, they'll do it to the nation, right?

REINER: Yes.

2000: You have to watch that. Yes.

REINER: So it's better that they dally with their wives or even on the outside.

2000: Let them have a mistress or two. Let 'em, 'cause they have to do it.

REINER: Sir, you are a virile human being.

2000: I hope to God.

REINER: You had many wives.

2000: You bet your boots, kid.

REINER: You had four hundred wives, was it?

2000: Four hundred-five hundred wives, I can't...countless, countless wives.

REINER: How many of those marriages were happy marriages?

2000: Seventy-one percent perfect. And the other ones — troubles, squabbles, and scrabbles and fights.

REINER: What was it about those marriages?

2000: Well, I mean — "Don't eat your soup with a fork" — you know, all of that stuff. And only one really bad thing. One runaway. I had a runaway.

REINER: Of all those four hundred wives, only one wife ran away?

2000: Yeah, Zenobia. She took off on me.

REINER: Why?

2000: We lived in Venice...

REINER: And?

2000: And a fellow come by, Lord Byron.

REINER: Oh.

2000: Good-looking guy.

REINER: Romantic poet.

2000: I'm telling you, good-looking. He said, "Hark, I hear..."

REINER: Oh, he started reciting poetry and your wife was there.

2000: "Hark, the ode..." "Hark..." "Hark..." He harked her right out of my life. She ran away with him. I think he's still harking her, to tell you the truth.

REINER: Do you remember her name?

2000: Zenobia.

REINER: The only Zenobia I know is the company that makes pistachio nuts.

2000: Well, they named it after her. She was very short and a little greenish and a little nutty.

REINER: How many children have you had? You said you counted once.

2000: Forty-two thousand children.

REINER: Forty-two thousand children?

2000: And not one comes to visit me.

REINER: They still haven't visited you?

2000: No.

REINER: I don't believe it, sir, because—

2000: Twenty-one thousand doctors.

REINER: Twenty-one thousand doctors?

2000: Twenty-one thousand doctors we turned out.

REINER: No kidding?

2000: Yes, sir.

REINER: How many accountants?

2000: Oh, at least seven hundred.

REINER: How many entertainers?

2000: Two.

REINER: Who are they? Are they famous? Do we know them?

2000: Boom-Boom Crosby.

REINER: Bing Crosby?

2000: Boom-Boom Crosby.

REINER: Oh, way back.

2000: Way back.

REINER: Did he sing?

2000: You want to hear how he sang?

REINER: Could you impersonate him?

2000: "Do da de do da de da de da...oh, browwwwnnnn do da de da..."

REINER: Sounds very much like Bing.

2000: Well, that's where he got it from. From Boom-Boom.

REINER: One of your sons was the originator of that kind of singing?

2000: Yes. He was terrific. Oh, sure. He made a dollar. He made a few bucks. He was all right. He gave us all his awards. We kept them in the cave. He was good to us. All the Jewish entertainers give their mothers and fathers the awards. They don't keep 'em in the house.

REINER: Moses?

2000: Moses gave his tablets.

REINER: He gave the tablets to his parents?

2000: Gave the tablets to his mother and father. Yes, sir. Over the mantlepiece. Oh, they're beautiful. And the TV man comes and he—"Oh, look, oh!"—they show them off. Yes. They're beautiful. Sure. They're very proud of them. And they have a forty-dollar frame around them. Beautiful. Gold leaf! Oh, perfect!

REINER: You made the statement that none of your children ever came to visit you? Do you ever visit any of them? Why don't you visit them?

2000: Sometimes I go to them and I...

REINER: You stand outside the door?

2000: Yeah, I don't like to go in. I'm all right. I'm comfortable in the rain. I don't have to sit down. I'm fine.

REINER: You're just like your father.

2000: We mock the thing we are to be.

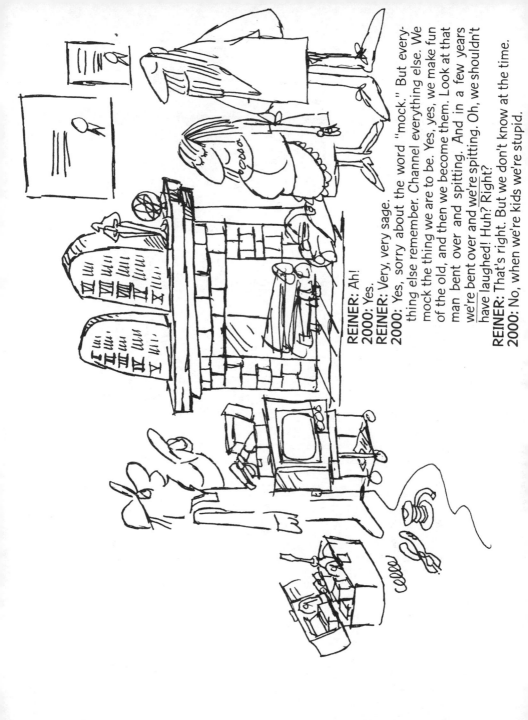

REINER: Ah!

2000: Yes.

REINER: Very, very sage.

2000: Yes, sorry about the word "mock." But everything else remember. Channel everything else. We mock the thing we are to be. Yes, yes, we make fun of the old, and then we become them. Look at that man bent over and spitting. And in a few years we're bent over and we're spitting. Oh, we shouldn't have laughed! Huh? Right?

REINER: That's right. But we don't know at the time.

2000: No, when we're kids we're stupid.

REINER: Sir, do you agree that Al Jolson was the greatest performer that ever walked on a stage?

2000: You know, Jolson was better on the telephone than he was singing.

REINER: I don't understand.

2000: Oh, fantastic telephone caller! I was present when he called Irving Berlin. He was in New York, Irving Berlin was in California. Calling long-distance. He needed a song for a new film he was making. *The Jazz Singer* or something.

REINER: *Jazz Singer*...

2000: So he called New York...

REINER: ...history-making film.

2000: Oh! He called New York. "Hello? Hello, New York? I would like to talk to Irving Berlin. Hello? Hello, is this Irving? Irving, this is Jolie! Irving!"

REINER: And what did he ask for?

2000: He wanted a song from him.

REINER: And what did he get from him?

2000: Irving wasn't there. "Hello? Irving? Irving! Are you Irving? Would you please put on Irving Berlin? I'm calling long-distance!" This was a big call. Paying a lot of money.

REINER: I see.

2000: "Hello, Irving? Ah, hello, Irving—Jolie! Yeah, this is Jolie, Irving! Listen, Irving, listen, Irving, I need a new song! Hello, is this Irving? Hello? Don't fool around! This is a forty-dollar call! This is Jolie, Irving! Irving!" He couldn't get him. Do you know what I mean? He couldn't get him.

REINER: Our nation now, sir, our nation is in a serious economic situation...

2000: Yes.

REINER: We have inflation, the balance of payments...

2000: Oh, boy.
REINER: The balance of trade...
2000: Ohhhh, boy!
REINER: The deficits...
2000: Oh, boy.
REINER: What would you suggest...
2000: Woof!
REINER: ...knowing what you do....
2000: Woof!
REINER: ...about the history...
2000: Woof!
REINER: ...of the economy....
2000: Woof! Are we in trouble!
REINER: ...of the world....
2000: I'm saying woof 'cause America's at low ebb now. We're at low ebb.
REINER: I know.
2000: The socioeconomic problems that we are faced with, the magnitude of them...
REINER: I know. I am asking you for help and a solution, if you have one.
2000: I have one solution.
REINER: Yes?
2000: I say this is the time to sell America. Sell it!
REINER: To whom? Sell America to whom?
2000: I'd say sell it to Japan. They're going to get it in ten years anyway, we might as well sell and make a profit.
REINER: And that's your solution to our economic problems?
2000: Yes, that's my solution.
REINER: I don't think it's a valid one, sir.
2000: Well, I didn't major in that in school.

REINER: Sir, do you feel there's any hope for the world?

2000: No. As long as the world is turning and spinning, we're gonna be dizzy and we're gonna make mistakes. If some smart guy can stop it so we're not nauseous, then we'll be able to think and we'll solve the problems of the world. Thank you and good night.